COMPANY DETAILS

COMPANY NAME

ADDRESS

E-MAIL ADDRESS

WEBSITE

PHONE   FAX

EMERGENCY CONTACT PERSON

PHONE   FAX

LOG BOOK DETAILS

CONTINUED FROM LOG BOOK

LOG START DATE

CONTINUED TO LOG BOOK

LOG END DATE

Volunteer Log Book

Name ....

Address ....

....

Phone ....

E-mail ....

Organization ....

Supervisor ....

Start Date .... End Date ....

DATE	HOURS	VOLUNTEER ACTIVITY	SUPERVISOR SIGN
TOTAL HOURS VOLUNTEERED			

Volunteer Log Book

Name ....

Address ....

....

Phone ....

E-mail ....

Organization ....

Supervisor ....

Start Date .... End Date ....

DATE	HOURS	VOLUNTEER ACTIVITY	SUPERVISOR SIGN
TOTAL HOURS VOLUNTEERED			

Volunteer Log Book

Name ....

Address ....

....

Phone ....

E-mail ....

Organization ....

Supervisor ....

Start Date .... End Date ....

DATE	HOURS	VOLUNTEER ACTIVITY	SUPERVISOR SIGN
TOTAL HOURS VOLUNTEERED			

Volunteer Log Book

Name ....

Address ....

....

Phone ....

E-mail ....

Organization ....

Supervisor ....

Start Date .... End Date ....

DATE	HOURS	VOLUNTEER ACTIVITY	SUPERVISOR SIGN
TOTAL HOURS VOLUNTEERED			

Volunteer Log Book

Name ....

Address ....

....

Phone ....

E-mail ....

Organization ....

Supervisor ....

Start Date .... End Date ....

DATE	HOURS	VOLUNTEER ACTIVITY	SUPERVISOR SIGN
TOTAL HOURS VOLUNTEERED			

Volunteer Log Book

Name ....

Address ....

....

Phone ....

E-mail ....

Organization ....

Supervisor ....

Start Date .... End Date ....

DATE	HOURS	VOLUNTEER ACTIVITY	SUPERVISOR SIGN
	TOTAL HOURS VOLUNTEERED		

Volunteer Log Book

Name ....
Address ....
....
Phone ....
E-mail ....
Organization ....
Supervisor ....
Start Date .... End Date ....

DATE	HOURS	VOLUNTEER ACTIVITY	SUPERVISOR SIGN
TOTAL HOURS VOLUNTEERED			

Volunteer Log Book

Name ....

Address ....

....

Phone ....

E-mail ....

Organization ....

Supervisor ....

Start Date .... End Date ....

DATE	HOURS	VOLUNTEER ACTIVITY	SUPERVISOR SIGN
	TOTAL HOURS VOLUNTEERED		

Volunteer Log Book

Name ....

Address ....

....

Phone ....

E-mail ....

Organization ....

Supervisor ....

Start Date .... End Date ....

DATE	HOURS	VOLUNTEER ACTIVITY	SUPERVISOR SIGN
TOTAL HOURS VOLUNTEERED			

Volunteer Log Book

Name ....

Address ....

....

Phone ....

E-mail ....

Organization ....

Supervisor ....

Start Date .... End Date ....

DATE	HOURS	VOLUNTEER ACTIVITY	SUPERVISOR SIGN
TOTAL HOURS VOLUNTEERED			

Volunteer Log Book

Name ....
Address ....
....
Phone ....
E-mail ....
Organization ....
Supervisor ....
Start Date .... End Date ....

DATE	HOURS	VOLUNTEER ACTIVITY	SUPERVISOR SIGN
TOTAL HOURS VOLUNTEERED			

Volunteer Log Book

Name ....

Address ....

....

Phone ....

E-mail ....

Organization ....

Supervisor ....

Start Date .... End Date ....

DATE	HOURS	VOLUNTEER ACTIVITY	SUPERVISOR SIGN
TOTAL HOURS VOLUNTEERED			

Volunteer Log Book

Name ....

Address ....

....

Phone ....

E-mail ....

Organization ....

Supervisor ....

Start Date .... End Date ....

DATE	HOURS	VOLUNTEER ACTIVITY	SUPERVISOR SIGN
TOTAL HOURS VOLUNTEERED			

Volunteer Log Book

Name ....

Address ....

....

Phone ....

E-mail ....

Organization ....

Supervisor ....

Start Date .... End Date ....

DATE	HOURS	VOLUNTEER ACTIVITY	SUPERVISOR SIGN
TOTAL HOURS VOLUNTEERED			

Volunteer Log Book

Name ....

Address ....

....

Phone ....

E-mail ....

Organization ....

Supervisor ....

Start Date .... End Date ....

DATE	HOURS	VOLUNTEER ACTIVITY	SUPERVISOR SIGN
TOTAL HOURS VOLUNTEERED			

Volunteer Log Book

Name ....

Address ....

....

Phone ....

E-mail ....

Organization ....

Supervisor ....

Start Date .... End Date ....

DATE	HOURS	VOLUNTEER ACTIVITY	SUPERVISOR SIGN
TOTAL HOURS VOLUNTEERED			

Volunteer Log Book

Name ....

Address ....

....

Phone ....

E-mail ....

Organization ....

Supervisor ....

Start Date .... End Date ....

DATE	HOURS	VOLUNTEER ACTIVITY	SUPERVISOR SIGN
TOTAL HOURS VOLUNTEERED			

Volunteer Log Book

Name ....

Address ....

....

Phone ....

E-mail ....

Organization ....

Supervisor ....

Start Date .... End Date ....

DATE	HOURS	VOLUNTEER ACTIVITY	SUPERVISOR SIGN
TOTAL HOURS VOLUNTEERED			

Volunteer Log Book

Name ....

Address ....

....

Phone ....

E-mail ....

Organization ....

Supervisor ....

Start Date .... End Date ....

DATE	HOURS	VOLUNTEER ACTIVITY	SUPERVISOR SIGN
TOTAL HOURS VOLUNTEERED			

Volunteer Log Book

Name ....

Address ....

....

Phone ....

E-mail ....

Organization ....

Supervisor ....

Start Date ....   End Date ....

DATE	HOURS	VOLUNTEER ACTIVITY	SUPERVISOR SIGN
TOTAL HOURS VOLUNTEERED			

Volunteer Log Book

Name ....

Address ....

....

Phone ....

E-mail ....

Organization ....

Supervisor ....

Start Date ....   End Date ....

DATE	HOURS	VOLUNTEER ACTIVITY	SUPERVISOR SIGN
TOTAL HOURS VOLUNTEERED			

Volunteer Log Book

Name ....

Address ....

....

Phone ....

E-mail ....

Organization ....

Supervisor ....

Start Date .... End Date ....

DATE	HOURS	VOLUNTEER ACTIVITY	SUPERVISOR SIGN
	TOTAL HOURS VOLUNTEERED		

Volunteer Log Book

Name ....

Address ....

....

Phone ....

E-mail ....

Organization ....

Supervisor ....

Start Date .... End Date ....

DATE	HOURS	VOLUNTEER ACTIVITY	SUPERVISOR SIGN
	TOTAL HOURS VOLUNTEERED		

Volunteer Log Book

Name ....

Address ....

....

Phone ....

E-mail ....

Organization ....

Supervisor ....

Start Date .... End Date ....

DATE	HOURS	VOLUNTEER ACTIVITY	SUPERVISOR SIGN
TOTAL HOURS VOLUNTEERED			

Volunteer Log Book

Name ....

Address ....

....

Phone ....

E-mail ....

Organization ....

Supervisor ....

Start Date .... End Date ....

DATE	HOURS	VOLUNTEER ACTIVITY	SUPERVISOR SIGN
TOTAL HOURS VOLUNTEERED			

Volunteer Log Book

Name ....

Address ....

....

Phone ....

E-mail ....

Organization ....

Supervisor ....

Start Date .... End Date ....

DATE	HOURS	VOLUNTEER ACTIVITY	SUPERVISOR SIGN
	TOTAL HOURS VOLUNTEERED		

Volunteer Log Book

Name ....

Address ....

....

Phone ....

E-mail ....

Organization ....

Supervisor ....

Start Date .... End Date ....

DATE	HOURS	VOLUNTEER ACTIVITY	SUPERVISOR SIGN
TOTAL HOURS VOLUNTEERED			

Volunteer Log Book

Name ....

Address ....

....

Phone ....

E-mail ....

Organization ....

Supervisor ....

Start Date .... End Date ....

DATE	HOURS	VOLUNTEER ACTIVITY	SUPERVISOR SIGN
TOTAL HOURS VOLUNTEERED			

Volunteer Log Book

Name ....
Address ....
....
Phone ....
E-mail ....
Organization ....
Supervisor ....
Start Date .... End Date ....

DATE	HOURS	VOLUNTEER ACTIVITY	SUPERVISOR SIGN
TOTAL HOURS VOLUNTEERED			

Volunteer Log Book

Name ....

Address ....

....

Phone ....

E-mail ....

Organization ....

Supervisor ....

Start Date .... End Date ....

DATE	HOURS	VOLUNTEER ACTIVITY	SUPERVISOR SIGN
TOTAL HOURS VOLUNTEERED			

Volunteer Log Book

Name ....

Address ....

....

Phone ....

E-mail ....

Organization ....

Supervisor ....

Start Date ....   End Date ....

DATE	HOURS	VOLUNTEER ACTIVITY	SUPERVISOR SIGN
TOTAL HOURS VOLUNTEERED			

Volunteer Log Book

Name ....

Address ....

....

Phone ....

E-mail ....

Organization ....

Supervisor ....

Start Date .... End Date ....

DATE	HOURS	VOLUNTEER ACTIVITY	SUPERVISOR SIGN
TOTAL HOURS VOLUNTEERED			

Volunteer Log Book

Name ....

Address ....

....

Phone ....

E-mail ....

Organization ....

Supervisor ....

Start Date .... End Date ....

DATE	HOURS	VOLUNTEER ACTIVITY	SUPERVISOR SIGN
TOTAL HOURS VOLUNTEERED			

Volunteer Log Book

Name ....

Address ....

....

Phone ....

E-mail ....

Organization ....

Supervisor ....

Start Date .... End Date ....

DATE	HOURS	VOLUNTEER ACTIVITY	SUPERVISOR SIGN
	TOTAL HOURS VOLUNTEERED		

Volunteer Log Book

Name ....

Address ....

....

Phone ....

E-mail ....

Organization ....

Supervisor ....

Start Date .... End Date ....

DATE	HOURS	VOLUNTEER ACTIVITY	SUPERVISOR SIGN
	TOTAL HOURS VOLUNTEERED		

Volunteer Log Book

Name ....

Address ....

....

Phone ....

E-mail ....

Organization ....

Supervisor ....

Start Date .... End Date ....

DATE	HOURS	VOLUNTEER ACTIVITY	SUPERVISOR SIGN
TOTAL HOURS VOLUNTEERED			

Volunteer Log Book

Name ....

Address ....

....

Phone ....

E-mail ....

Organization ....

Supervisor ....

Start Date .... End Date ....

DATE	HOURS	VOLUNTEER ACTIVITY	SUPERVISOR SIGN
TOTAL HOURS VOLUNTEERED			

Volunteer Log Book

Name ....

Address ....

....

Phone ....

E-mail ....

Organization ....

Supervisor ....

Start Date .... End Date ....

DATE	HOURS	VOLUNTEER ACTIVITY	SUPERVISOR SIGN
TOTAL HOURS VOLUNTEERED			

Volunteer Log Book

Name ....

Address ....

....

Phone ....

E-mail ....

Organization ....

Supervisor ....

Start Date .... End Date ....

DATE	HOURS	VOLUNTEER ACTIVITY	SUPERVISOR SIGN
TOTAL HOURS VOLUNTEERED			

Volunteer Log Book

Name ....
Address ....
....
Phone ....
E-mail ....
Organization ....
Supervisor ....
Start Date .... End Date ....

DATE	HOURS	VOLUNTEER ACTIVITY	SUPERVISOR SIGN
TOTAL HOURS VOLUNTEERED			

Volunteer Log Book

Name ....

Address ....

....

Phone ....

E-mail ....

Organization ....

Supervisor ....

Start Date .... End Date ....

DATE	HOURS	VOLUNTEER ACTIVITY	SUPERVISOR SIGN
TOTAL HOURS VOLUNTEERED			

Volunteer Log Book

Name ....

Address ....

....

Phone ....

E-mail ....

Organization ....

Supervisor ....

Start Date .... End Date ....

DATE	HOURS	VOLUNTEER ACTIVITY	SUPERVISOR SIGN
	TOTAL HOURS VOLUNTEERED		

Volunteer Log Book

Name ....

Address ....

....

Phone ....

E-mail ....

Organization ....

Supervisor ....

Start Date .... End Date ....

DATE	HOURS	VOLUNTEER ACTIVITY	SUPERVISOR SIGN
TOTAL HOURS VOLUNTEERED			

Volunteer Log Book

Name ....

Address ....

....

Phone ....

E-mail ....

Organization ....

Supervisor ....

Start Date .... End Date ....

DATE	HOURS	VOLUNTEER ACTIVITY	SUPERVISOR SIGN
TOTAL HOURS VOLUNTEERED			

Volunteer Log Book

Name ....
Address ....
....
Phone ....
E-mail ....
Organization ....
Supervisor ....
Start Date .... End Date ....

DATE	HOURS	VOLUNTEER ACTIVITY	SUPERVISOR SIGN
TOTAL HOURS VOLUNTEERED			

Volunteer Log Book

Name ....
Address ....
....
Phone ....
E-mail ....
Organization ....
Supervisor ....
Start Date .... End Date ....

DATE	HOURS	VOLUNTEER ACTIVITY	SUPERVISOR SIGN
TOTAL HOURS VOLUNTEERED			

Volunteer Log Book

Name ....

Address ....

....

Phone ....

E-mail ....

Organization ....

Supervisor ....

Start Date .... End Date ....

DATE	HOURS	VOLUNTEER ACTIVITY	SUPERVISOR SIGN
TOTAL HOURS VOLUNTEERED			

Volunteer Log Book

Name ....

Address ....

....

Phone ....

E-mail ....

Organization ....

Supervisor ....

Start Date .... End Date ....

DATE	HOURS	VOLUNTEER ACTIVITY	SUPERVISOR SIGN
TOTAL HOURS VOLUNTEERED			

Volunteer Log Book

Name ....
Address ....
....
Phone ....
E-mail ....
Organization ....
Supervisor ....
Start Date .... End Date ....

DATE	HOURS	VOLUNTEER ACTIVITY	SUPERVISOR SIGN
TOTAL HOURS VOLUNTEERED			

Volunteer Log Book

Name ....

Address ....

....

Phone ....

E-mail ....

Organization ....

Supervisor ....

Start Date .... End Date ....

DATE	HOURS	VOLUNTEER ACTIVITY	SUPERVISOR SIGN
TOTAL HOURS VOLUNTEERED			

Volunteer Log Book

Name ....

Address ....

....

Phone ....

E-mail ....

Organization ....

Supervisor ....

Start Date .... End Date ....

DATE	HOURS	VOLUNTEER ACTIVITY	SUPERVISOR SIGN
TOTAL HOURS VOLUNTEERED			

Volunteer Log Book

Name ....

Address ....

....

Phone ....

E-mail ....

Organization ....

Supervisor ....

Start Date .... End Date ....

DATE	HOURS	VOLUNTEER ACTIVITY	SUPERVISOR SIGN
TOTAL HOURS VOLUNTEERED			

Volunteer Log Book

Name ....
Address ....
....
Phone ....
E-mail ....
Organization ....
Supervisor ....
Start Date .... End Date ....

DATE	HOURS	VOLUNTEER ACTIVITY	SUPERVISOR SIGN
TOTAL HOURS VOLUNTEERED			

Volunteer Log Book

Name ....

Address ....

....

Phone ....

E-mail ....

Organization ....

Supervisor ....

Start Date .... End Date ....

DATE	HOURS	VOLUNTEER ACTIVITY	SUPERVISOR SIGN
TOTAL HOURS VOLUNTEERED			

Volunteer Log Book

Name ....

Address ....

....

Phone ....

E-mail ....

Organization ....

Supervisor ....

Start Date .... End Date ....

DATE	HOURS	VOLUNTEER ACTIVITY	SUPERVISOR SIGN
TOTAL HOURS VOLUNTEERED			

Volunteer Log Book

Name ....

Address ....

....

Phone ....

E-mail ....

Organization ....

Supervisor ....

Start Date .... End Date ....

DATE	HOURS	VOLUNTEER ACTIVITY	SUPERVISOR SIGN
TOTAL HOURS VOLUNTEERED			

Volunteer Log Book

Name ....

Address ....

....

Phone ....

E-mail ....

Organization ....

Supervisor ....

Start Date .... End Date ....

DATE	HOURS	VOLUNTEER ACTIVITY	SUPERVISOR SIGN
TOTAL HOURS VOLUNTEERED			

Volunteer Log Book

Name ....

Address ....

....

Phone ....

E-mail ....

Organization ....

Supervisor ....

Start Date .... End Date ....

DATE	HOURS	VOLUNTEER ACTIVITY	SUPERVISOR SIGN
TOTAL HOURS VOLUNTEERED			

Volunteer Log Book

Name ....

Address ....
....

Phone ....

E-mail ....

Organization ....

Supervisor ....

Start Date .... End Date ....

DATE	HOURS	VOLUNTEER ACTIVITY	SUPERVISOR SIGN
TOTAL HOURS VOLUNTEERED			

Volunteer Log Book

Name ....

Address ....

....

Phone ....

E-mail ....

Organization ....

Supervisor ....

Start Date .... End Date ....

DATE	HOURS	VOLUNTEER ACTIVITY	SUPERVISOR SIGN
	TOTAL HOURS VOLUNTEERED		

Volunteer Log Book

Name ....

Address ....

....

Phone ....

E-mail ....

Organization ....

Supervisor ....

Start Date .... End Date ....

DATE	HOURS	VOLUNTEER ACTIVITY	SUPERVISOR SIGN
TOTAL HOURS VOLUNTEERED			

Volunteer Log Book

Name ....

Address ....

....

Phone ....

E-mail ....

Organization ....

Supervisor ....

Start Date .... End Date ....

DATE	HOURS	VOLUNTEER ACTIVITY	SUPERVISOR SIGN
	TOTAL HOURS VOLUNTEERED		

Volunteer Log Book

Name ....

Address ....

....

Phone ....

E-mail ....

Organization ....

Supervisor ....

Start Date .... End Date ....

DATE	HOURS	VOLUNTEER ACTIVITY	SUPERVISOR SIGN
TOTAL HOURS VOLUNTEERED			

Volunteer Log Book

Name ....

Address ....

....

Phone ....

E-mail ....

Organization ....

Supervisor ....

Start Date .... End Date ....

DATE	HOURS	VOLUNTEER ACTIVITY	SUPERVISOR SIGN
TOTAL HOURS VOLUNTEERED			

Volunteer Log Book

Name ....

Address ....

....

Phone ....

E-mail ....

Organization ....

Supervisor ....

Start Date .... End Date ....

DATE	HOURS	VOLUNTEER ACTIVITY	SUPERVISOR SIGN
TOTAL HOURS VOLUNTEERED			

Volunteer Log Book

Name ....

Address ....

....

Phone ....

E-mail ....

Organization ....

Supervisor ....

Start Date .... End Date ....

DATE	HOURS	VOLUNTEER ACTIVITY	SUPERVISOR SIGN
TOTAL HOURS VOLUNTEERED			

Volunteer Log Book

Name ....

Address ....

....

Phone ....

E-mail ....

Organization ....

Supervisor ....

Start Date .... End Date ....

DATE	HOURS	VOLUNTEER ACTIVITY	SUPERVISOR SIGN
TOTAL HOURS VOLUNTEERED			

Volunteer Log Book

Name ....

Address ....

....

Phone ....

E-mail ....

Organization ....

Supervisor ....

Start Date .... End Date ....

DATE	HOURS	VOLUNTEER ACTIVITY	SUPERVISOR SIGN
TOTAL HOURS VOLUNTEERED			

Volunteer Log Book

Name ....

Address ....

....

Phone ....

E-mail ....

Organization ....

Supervisor ....

Start Date .... End Date ....

DATE	HOURS	VOLUNTEER ACTIVITY	SUPERVISOR SIGN
TOTAL HOURS VOLUNTEERED			

Volunteer Log Book

Name ....

Address ....

....

Phone ....

E-mail ....

Organization ....

Supervisor ....

Start Date .... End Date ....

DATE	HOURS	VOLUNTEER ACTIVITY	SUPERVISOR SIGN
TOTAL HOURS VOLUNTEERED			

Volunteer Log Book

Name ....

Address ....

....

Phone ....

E-mail ....

Organization ....

Supervisor ....

Start Date .... End Date ....

DATE	HOURS	VOLUNTEER ACTIVITY	SUPERVISOR SIGN
TOTAL HOURS VOLUNTEERED			

Volunteer Log Book

Name ....

Address ....

....

Phone ....

E-mail ....

Organization ....

Supervisor ....

Start Date .... End Date ....

DATE	HOURS	VOLUNTEER ACTIVITY	SUPERVISOR SIGN
TOTAL HOURS VOLUNTEERED			

Volunteer Log Book

Name ....
Address ....
....
Phone ....
E-mail ....
Organization ....
Supervisor ....
Start Date .... End Date ....

DATE	HOURS	VOLUNTEER ACTIVITY	SUPERVISOR SIGN
TOTAL HOURS VOLUNTEERED			

Volunteer Log Book

Name ....

Address ....

....

Phone ....

E-mail ....

Organization ....

Supervisor ....

Start Date .... End Date ....

DATE	HOURS	VOLUNTEER ACTIVITY	SUPERVISOR SIGN
	TOTAL HOURS VOLUNTEERED		

Volunteer Log Book

Name ....

Address ....

....

Phone ....

E-mail ....

Organization ....

Supervisor ....

Start Date .... End Date ....

DATE	HOURS	VOLUNTEER ACTIVITY	SUPERVISOR SIGN
TOTAL HOURS VOLUNTEERED			

Volunteer Log Book

Name ....

Address ....

....

Phone ....

E-mail ....

Organization ....

Supervisor ....

Start Date .... End Date ....

DATE	HOURS	VOLUNTEER ACTIVITY	SUPERVISOR SIGN
TOTAL HOURS VOLUNTEERED			

Volunteer Log Book

Name ....

Address ....

....

Phone ....

E-mail ....

Organization ....

Supervisor ....

Start Date .... End Date ....

DATE	HOURS	VOLUNTEER ACTIVITY	SUPERVISOR SIGN
TOTAL HOURS VOLUNTEERED			

Volunteer Log Book

Name ....

Address ....

....

Phone ....

E-mail ....

Organization ....

Supervisor ....

Start Date .... End Date ....

DATE	HOURS	VOLUNTEER ACTIVITY	SUPERVISOR SIGN
TOTAL HOURS VOLUNTEERED			

Volunteer Log Book

Name ....

Address ....

....

Phone ....

E-mail ....

Organization ....

Supervisor ....

Start Date .... End Date ....

DATE	HOURS	VOLUNTEER ACTIVITY	SUPERVISOR SIGN
TOTAL HOURS VOLUNTEERED			

Volunteer Log Book

Name ....

Address ....

....

Phone ....

E-mail ....

Organization ....

Supervisor ....

Start Date .... End Date ....

DATE	HOURS	VOLUNTEER ACTIVITY	SUPERVISOR SIGN
TOTAL HOURS VOLUNTEERED			

Volunteer Log Book

Name ....

Address ....

....

Phone ....

E-mail ....

Organization ....

Supervisor ....

Start Date .... End Date ....

DATE	HOURS	VOLUNTEER ACTIVITY	SUPERVISOR SIGN
TOTAL HOURS VOLUNTEERED			

Volunteer Log Book

Name ....

Address ....

....

Phone ....

E-mail ....

Organization ....

Supervisor ....

Start Date .... End Date ....

DATE	HOURS	VOLUNTEER ACTIVITY	SUPERVISOR SIGN
TOTAL HOURS VOLUNTEERED			

Volunteer Log Book

Name ....
Address ....
....

Phone ....
E-mail ....
Organization ....
Supervisor ....
Start Date .... End Date ....

DATE	HOURS	VOLUNTEER ACTIVITY	SUPERVISOR SIGN
TOTAL HOURS VOLUNTEERED			

Volunteer Log Book

Name ....

Address ....

....

Phone ....

E-mail ....

Organization ....

Supervisor ....

Start Date .... End Date ....

DATE	HOURS	VOLUNTEER ACTIVITY	SUPERVISOR SIGN
TOTAL HOURS VOLUNTEERED			

Volunteer Log Book

Name ....

Address ....

....

Phone ....

E-mail ....

Organization ....

Supervisor ....

Start Date .... End Date ....

DATE	HOURS	VOLUNTEER ACTIVITY	SUPERVISOR SIGN
TOTAL HOURS VOLUNTEERED			

Volunteer Log Book

Name ....

Address ....

....

Phone ....

E-mail ....

Organization ....

Supervisor ....

Start Date .... End Date ....

DATE	HOURS	VOLUNTEER ACTIVITY	SUPERVISOR SIGN
TOTAL HOURS VOLUNTEERED			

Volunteer Log Book

Name ....

Address ....

....

Phone ....

E-mail ....

Organization ....

Supervisor ....

Start Date .... End Date ....

DATE	HOURS	VOLUNTEER ACTIVITY	SUPERVISOR SIGN
TOTAL HOURS VOLUNTEERED			

Volunteer Log Book

Name ....

Address ....

....

Phone ....

E-mail ....

Organization ....

Supervisor ....

Start Date .... End Date ....

DATE	HOURS	VOLUNTEER ACTIVITY	SUPERVISOR SIGN
	TOTAL HOURS VOLUNTEERED		

Volunteer Log Book

Name ....

Address ....

....

Phone ....

E-mail ....

Organization ....

Supervisor ....

Start Date .... End Date ....

DATE	HOURS	VOLUNTEER ACTIVITY	SUPERVISOR SIGN
TOTAL HOURS VOLUNTEERED			

Volunteer Log Book

Name ....

Address ....

....

Phone ....

E-mail ....

Organization ....

Supervisor ....

Start Date .... End Date ....

DATE	HOURS	VOLUNTEER ACTIVITY	SUPERVISOR SIGN
TOTAL HOURS VOLUNTEERED			

Volunteer Log Book

Name ....

Address ....

....

Phone ....

E-mail ....

Organization ....

Supervisor ....

Start Date .... End Date ....

DATE	HOURS	VOLUNTEER ACTIVITY	SUPERVISOR SIGN
TOTAL HOURS VOLUNTEERED			

Volunteer Log Book

Name ....

Address ....

....

Phone ....

E-mail ....

Organization ....

Supervisor ....

Start Date .... End Date ....

DATE	HOURS	VOLUNTEER ACTIVITY	SUPERVISOR SIGN
TOTAL HOURS VOLUNTEERED			

Volunteer Log Book

Name ....

Address ....

....

Phone ....

E-mail ....

Organization ....

Supervisor ....

Start Date .... End Date ....

DATE	HOURS	VOLUNTEER ACTIVITY	SUPERVISOR SIGN
	TOTAL HOURS VOLUNTEERED		

Volunteer Log Book

Name ....

Address ....

....

Phone ....

E-mail ....

Organization ....

Supervisor ....

Start Date .... End Date ....

DATE	HOURS	VOLUNTEER ACTIVITY	SUPERVISOR SIGN
TOTAL HOURS VOLUNTEERED			

Volunteer Log Book

Name ....

Address ....

....

Phone ....

E-mail ....

Organization ....

Supervisor ....

Start Date .... End Date ....

DATE	HOURS	VOLUNTEER ACTIVITY	SUPERVISOR SIGN
TOTAL HOURS VOLUNTEERED			

Volunteer Log Book

Name ....

Address ....

....

Phone ....

E-mail ....

Organization ....

Supervisor ....

Start Date .... End Date ....

DATE	HOURS	VOLUNTEER ACTIVITY	SUPERVISOR SIGN
TOTAL HOURS VOLUNTEERED			

Volunteer Log Book

Name ....

Address ....
....

Phone ....

E-mail ....

Organization ....

Supervisor ....

Start Date .... End Date ....

DATE	HOURS	VOLUNTEER ACTIVITY	SUPERVISOR SIGN
TOTAL HOURS VOLUNTEERED			

Volunteer Log Book

Name ....

Address ....

....

Phone ....

E-mail ....

Organization ....

Supervisor ....

Start Date .... End Date ....

DATE	HOURS	VOLUNTEER ACTIVITY	SUPERVISOR SIGN
TOTAL HOURS VOLUNTEERED			

Volunteer Log Book

Name ....

Address ....

....

Phone ....

E-mail ....

Organization ....

Supervisor ....

Start Date .... End Date ....

DATE	HOURS	VOLUNTEER ACTIVITY	SUPERVISOR SIGN
TOTAL HOURS VOLUNTEERED			

Volunteer Log Book

Name ....

Address ....

....

Phone ....

E-mail ....

Organization ....

Supervisor ....

Start Date .... End Date ....

DATE	HOURS	VOLUNTEER ACTIVITY	SUPERVISOR SIGN
	TOTAL HOURS VOLUNTEERED		

Volunteer Log Book

Name ....

Address ....

....

Phone ....

E-mail ....

Organization ....

Supervisor ....

Start Date .... End Date ....

DATE	HOURS	VOLUNTEER ACTIVITY	SUPERVISOR SIGN
TOTAL HOURS VOLUNTEERED			

Volunteer Log Book

Name ....

Address ....

....

Phone ....

E-mail ....

Organization ....

Supervisor ....

Start Date .... End Date ....

DATE	HOURS	VOLUNTEER ACTIVITY	SUPERVISOR SIGN
TOTAL HOURS VOLUNTEERED			

Volunteer Log Book

Name ....

Address ....

....

Phone ....

E-mail ....

Organization ....

Supervisor ....

Start Date .... End Date ....

DATE	HOURS	VOLUNTEER ACTIVITY	SUPERVISOR SIGN
	TOTAL HOURS VOLUNTEERED		

Volunteer Log Book

Name ....

Address ....

....

Phone ....

E-mail ....

Organization ....

Supervisor ....

Start Date .... End Date ....

DATE	HOURS	VOLUNTEER ACTIVITY	SUPERVISOR SIGN
TOTAL HOURS VOLUNTEERED			

Volunteer Log Book

Name ....

Address ....

....

Phone ....

E-mail ....

Organization ....

Supervisor ....

Start Date .... End Date ....

DATE	HOURS	VOLUNTEER ACTIVITY	SUPERVISOR SIGN
TOTAL HOURS VOLUNTEERED			

Volunteer Log Book

Name ....

Address ....

....

Phone ....

E-mail ....

Organization ....

Supervisor ....

Start Date .... End Date ....

DATE	HOURS	VOLUNTEER ACTIVITY	SUPERVISOR SIGN
TOTAL HOURS VOLUNTEERED			

Volunteer Log Book

Name ....

Address ....

....

Phone ....

E-mail ....

Organization ....

Supervisor ....

Start Date .... End Date ....

DATE	HOURS	VOLUNTEER ACTIVITY	SUPERVISOR SIGN
TOTAL HOURS VOLUNTEERED			

Volunteer Log Book

Name ....

Address ....

....

Phone ....

E-mail ....

Organization ....

Supervisor ....

Start Date .... End Date ....

DATE	HOURS	VOLUNTEER ACTIVITY	SUPERVISOR SIGN
TOTAL HOURS VOLUNTEERED			

Volunteer Log Book

Name ....

Address ....

....

Phone ....

E-mail ....

Organization ....

Supervisor ....

Start Date .... End Date ....

DATE	HOURS	VOLUNTEER ACTIVITY	SUPERVISOR SIGN
TOTAL HOURS VOLUNTEERED			

Volunteer Log Book

Name ....

Address ....

....

Phone ....

E-mail ....

Organization ....

Supervisor ....

Start Date .... End Date ....

DATE	HOURS	VOLUNTEER ACTIVITY	SUPERVISOR SIGN
TOTAL HOURS VOLUNTEERED			

Volunteer Log Book

Name ....
Address ....
....
Phone ....
E-mail ....
Organization ....
Supervisor ....
Start Date .... End Date ....

DATE	HOURS	VOLUNTEER ACTIVITY	SUPERVISOR SIGN
TOTAL HOURS VOLUNTEERED			

Volunteer Log Book

Name ....
Address ....
....
Phone ....
E-mail ....
Organization ....
Supervisor ....
Start Date .... End Date ....

DATE	HOURS	VOLUNTEER ACTIVITY	SUPERVISOR SIGN
TOTAL HOURS VOLUNTEERED			

Volunteer Log Book

Name ....

Address ....

....

Phone ....

E-mail ....

Organization ....

Supervisor ....

Start Date .... End Date ....

DATE	HOURS	VOLUNTEER ACTIVITY	SUPERVISOR SIGN
TOTAL HOURS VOLUNTEERED			

Volunteer Log Book

Name ....

Address ....

....

Phone ....

E-mail ....

Organization ....

Supervisor ....

Start Date .... End Date ....

DATE	HOURS	VOLUNTEER ACTIVITY	SUPERVISOR SIGN
TOTAL HOURS VOLUNTEERED			

Volunteer Log Book

Name ....

Address ....

....

Phone ....

E-mail ....

Organization ....

Supervisor ....

Start Date .... End Date ....

DATE	HOURS	VOLUNTEER ACTIVITY	SUPERVISOR SIGN
TOTAL HOURS VOLUNTEERED			

Volunteer Log Book

Name ....

Address ....

....

Phone ....

E-mail ....

Organization ....

Supervisor ....

Start Date .... End Date ....

DATE	HOURS	VOLUNTEER ACTIVITY	SUPERVISOR SIGN
TOTAL HOURS VOLUNTEERED			

Volunteer Log Book

Name ....

Address ....

....

Phone ....

E-mail ....

Organization ....

Supervisor ....

Start Date .... End Date ....

DATE	HOURS	VOLUNTEER ACTIVITY	SUPERVISOR SIGN
TOTAL HOURS VOLUNTEERED			

Volunteer Log Book

Name ....

Address ....

....

Phone ....

E-mail ....

Organization ....

Supervisor ....

Start Date .... End Date ....

DATE	HOURS	VOLUNTEER ACTIVITY	SUPERVISOR SIGN
TOTAL HOURS VOLUNTEERED			

Volunteer Log Book

Name ....

Address ....

....

Phone ....

E-mail ....

Organization ....

Supervisor ....

Start Date .... End Date ....

DATE	HOURS	VOLUNTEER ACTIVITY	SUPERVISOR SIGN
TOTAL HOURS VOLUNTEERED			

CPSIA information can be obtained
at www.ICGtesting.com
Printed in the USA
BVHW070842240221
600901BV00009B/985